MW01277343

THE MOON KNOWS NO BOUNDARY

ESSENTIAL POETS SERIES 128

Canada Council
for the Arts

Conseil des Arts
du Canada

ONTARIO ARTS COUNCIL
CONSEIL DES ARTS DE L'ONTARIO

Guernica Editions Inc. acknowledges the support of The Canada Council for the Arts.
Guernica Editions Inc. acknowledges the support of the Ontario Arts Council.

MARY TILBERG

THE MOON KNOWS
NO BOUNDARY

P.R.
4/15/05
For Bob,
From Mary Tilberg

GUERNICA

TORONTO · BUFFALO · CHICAGO · LANCASTER (U.K.)
2004

Copyright © 2004, by Mary Tilberg and Guernica Editions Inc.
All rights reserved. The use of any part of this publication, reproduced, transmitted in any form
or by any means, electronic, mechanical, photocopying, recording or otherwise stored in a
retrieval system, without the prior consent of the publisher
is an infringement of the copyright law.

Antonio D'Alfonso, editor
Guernica Editions Inc.
P.O. Box 117, Station P, Toronto (ON), Canada M5S 2S6
2250 Military Road, Tonawanda, N.Y. 14150-6000 U.S.A.

Distributors:
University of Toronto Press Distribution,
5201 Dufferin Street, Toronto, (ON), Canada M3H 5T8

Gazelle Book Services, White Cross Mills, High Town, Lancaster LA1 1XS U.K.

Independent Publishers Group,
814 N. Franklin Street, Chicago, Il. 60610 U.S.A.

First edition.
Printed in Canada.

Legal Deposit – First Quarter
National Library of Canada
Library of Congress Catalog Card Number: 2003114601
National Library of Canada Cataloguing in Publication
Tilberg, Mary
The moon knows no boundary / Mary Tilberg.
(Essential poets series ; 128)
Poems.
ISBN 1 55071-105-7
I. Title. II. Series.
PS8589.I54M66 2004 C811'.6 C2003-906555-3

Contents

Acknowledgements

My far-flung family whose adventures on this earth inspired many of these poems; Banff Centre for the Arts for space and luxurious time; Dave Allen; special thanks to Don Coles, and to Chris Wisemen and Lola Tostevin; Anne Szumigalski and Adele Wiseman who remain inspirations; Steven Heighton and Mary Huggard for their feedback (persistent and insistent!) on the Varykino poems; many friends, especially Louise Young, Rachna Gilmore and Caroline Adderson, for their unflagging support; Miriam Abraham, who was there at the beginning. "Migrant" first appeared in *The Fiddlehead*.

In memory of Maria Salita

Siberian Snow

She tells us the last time
she ever saw her father –
beloved! she was spoiled! –
was in Khabarovsk, 1924,
just before she escaped to Harbin.

Rippling white across his chest,
his beard was a fan
of Siberian snow. This
she recalls, and his blue eyes,
much too bright.

Like a fragile hummingbird vibrating
oceans of air, my tiny grandmother,
whose waist once whispered
a mere circlet of two hands in the dance.
She remembers in a language I know only
in my arteries – Russian river.

Yet, as she celebrates the story,
relates how she went to the front
to see her father, I'm swept aboard that train
shrieking northwest in the moonlit steppes,
smoke shuddering back like wind-swept hair.

Near the battlefront her father Mikhail
looks up from battle reports, thunderstruck:
"Maria, in God's name!"
as he reaches out for her.

A Spy Story (1915)

At Odessa
they part at the station,
the tall engineer, his diminutive bride.
He worries she looks younger than eighteen.
Will she take their future safely back to Khabarovsk?

Maria waits until he's gone, to dry her eyes,
then hurries to cash in her Siberia ticket.
Stubborn, she has other plans.
Her father Mikhail missed the wedding,
so she will go to him on the Polish Front.

Night falls. Hidden beneath a greatcoat
on a troop train heading north. Days, nights.
 "No one will betray you, little sister."
She sleeps with the country wrapped around her

until one night, brakes screeching, the train halts
in the dark plain, the Front not far.
Officers yell, soldiers stir groggy,
hundreds of dreams blink out.

Maria awakes with a rush
of expectations, thrusts her face out
to ask: Where are we now?
Appalled, an officer challenges her.

Imagine her father, the general,
when hauled before him,
one slight, vociferous spy,
his only child.

How love dares journey
through such landscapes.

In Winter

In winter the child by the tracks
throws rotten potatoes. Trainmen
answer with chunks of coal.

Oh Russia awake.

He climbs up, hand over hand, this child
of the poor who craves knowledge
and respect like water and bread.

In pre-1917 Russia,
electrical engineers at a premium,
Vladimir, you've chosen well, your profession
and your wife; both will save your life.

On the Trans-Siberian he has his own car,
the telegraph his sacred duty. Wires vibrate
through the taiga, all Sibir now linked to the West.
What miracles of technology await us?

Awake, oh my Russia!

He stares at his large hands and remembers
the frozen child picking coal.

All along the greatest of railways he spreads
the word. A new day! A democratic Russia!

The vast taiga spreads out
into the new century,
until the day Kerensky tumbles,
until the slaughter of the Tsar.

Visions through a waterfall of blood.
His railcar speeds through Siberia
spreading the word: Arise, my poor Russians.

Aie, Vladimir, flee to Harbin with the others!
Be hungry in Shanghai. You think mere months.
Think of a lifetime.

Aie, Vladimir, poised on the roof in Shanghai,
your small children begging you to live.
You, with nothing left to throw.

Maria tells them: "Ignore him.
He won't jump."

Vladimir

Questions for my grandfather, 1883-1949

You must have loved your Russia more
than you ever did Maria and the children.
Why else remain stateless all your life,
exiled in China, feeding fury with your pen,
stoking the counter-revolution – cold furnace?

Such poverty! Your many children asleep
in beds of rags on the floor in
one room (Mama told me), while
Maria plotted their survival.

What a wife you had! What love
drove her, and what ingenuity
she had to survive you, after all,
and all of us with her. Did you
ever really see her, this little
hummingbird of a woman?

Australia! They needed your
engineering skills. You could've
boarded the ship that sailed
from that disaster, planted
your children in fresh soil, but no,
never ask me to desert Mother Russia!

What was it you loved so much?
Russia, giant thrusting out
into modernity, hands reaching
for the hoist up. The muscles
tensing, straining forward, were yours.

14

Yet what could you do, sorry exile?

How often you'd travelled west to east,
Trans-Siberia and back. Each time
you close your eyes, is it geography
you see? The snowy steppes below the moon?
The vast taiga buzzing in the spring?

Like Lermontov, an unreasonable love
for native land... smoke rising from
sad villages, chill smell of snow...

As you walk about Shanghai, Father,
days of exile lengthening to years,
is it the streets of Moscow that you walk?
Petersburg? The small village of your folks
in Belorus? Or those streets of your youth
in Odessa? Khabarovsk claims your trance,
perhaps. You are distant from us.

The music of the language you couldn't
forsake, Pushkin, Tolstoy. The Easter
Liturgy, candles carried in the snowy
streets on Christmas Eve. All like
an endless river in your veins without
which you'd wither. Was it ego?
How could you admit defeat?
English syllables grated your ears,
but Maria insisted on the future.
French! English! How quickly
the children learned!
A veritable Babel. You shuddered
to think. Your brilliant kids,
flower seeds on the wind.

And all the while Maria plotted –
scraped and scrimped and schemed –
our survival. We live because of her.

You must have loved your Russia more
than you ever loved us,
this mistress who stole away
our father's deepest affections.

Be happy, old spirit.
Your great love, bleeding, tattered,
dragging herself along the snowy streets,
is nevertheless alive.
Nichevo . . .

Your children bloom elsewhere.

Boot Hill

Sometimes he saw American sailors
pay the rickshaw coolies well. At one end
of an alleyway the thin Chinese men stood
aside as burly sailors lined the rickshaws
up at the other, waited for the signal to begin
their race. A rickshaw derby! Lay your bets, boys!
They could hardly stand for laughing.

They posed for pictures, their arms flung about each
other, draped over the shafts of the rickshaws. The slight
half-starved coolies bowed and bobbed, smiling, smiling.

The streets of Shanghai swarmed with Yankee sailors.
Vladimir forbade his many daughters even a glance
at these rowdy boys, not even a slight lift of a brow.
He didn't like Americans much.
Emigrate there? Never!

Poor Grandfather.
Weeks after fleeing China, 1949,
you lay dying of cancer,
a San Francisco hospital
draining away your life savings,
all gone before the final slice
of the scalpel.

If I could I would take your bones
out of Boot Hill, that vast San Francisco
suburb of the dead, and bury them
under the birches in a quiet wood
somewhere near Smolensk.

Maria (1992)

*The fact that of our Russian heritage the hardi-
est survivor proved to be a traveling bag is both
logical and emblematic.*
Vladimir Nabokov, *Speak, Memory*

I

A paean for Maria!
My tiny Baba, so elegant.
If only I could've spoken with you,
the language like the Volga
in flood between us.
All my life I will hear
your rich ironic Russian,
remember your low chuckle.

Tell us another story, tell us.
Katya or Natasha will interpret.
Please, just a while more,
though I know how you're longing to go.

II

She sits by the window in the morning
gazing up at the hills of Santa Barbara.
Sunlight just misses her face.
What do you think of, Grandma?
Pensive. Of the past?
Whether tonight you will go at last?
I can approach you only on paper.
The present submerges in the past,
vies with ninety-five years.
No contest: You sit mostly silent now,
your eyes allow no more knitting,

no reading, give the inner
vision precedence.

Perhaps you think of the Napa Valley,
Old Russia in the voices of friends,
incense & music in the small domed church
beneath the sycamores,

or the years in San Francisco, your boarding house
on Seventh Avenue near Golden Gate.

So many places compete!
Maybe you're in Venezuela, the house
with the walled garden
full of your children and their children
in noisy refuge.

You look away from the window at Katya
slicing vegetables at the sink. Do you recall
her at seventeen? You in Venezuela already,
and she stuck in the DP camp, Philippines,
where she buried her firstborn son?

How can we ever know the right from the wrong
road to go? Do you carry the guilt? The load . . .

And maybe you are only thinking now
of what Katya will prepare for dinner.

III

Inevitable.

Sitting together,
they talk about everything, yet nothing.
Maria listens, says little.

Suddenly she slumps against one of them,
pales, so pale the daughters are afraid.
"Mama, what is it? Why do you cry?"
She shakes her head, doesn't know.
Involuntary response, so the doctor says,
to the slight stroke she's just suffered,
minor rehearsal, aftermark
of too much life.

IV

From across the world they have come.
She looks at them gathered around her bed.
So many jokes and stories fly about the room,
and any sad eyes are quickly averted.
"Ah, this is the most difficult part,"
she says aloud. "To see you all again.
To see you leave."

V

Late afternoon Maria naps and dreams of Shanghai,
Rue Molière in the French Concession,
shrill voices clamouring in the streets, the humid
summer nights, scarlet fever, Olga
in the tiny plot of Chinese earth.

Evening. She sits under the rose trellis
breathing air spiced oranges and figs.

Katya weeds the flowers.

Tsingtao, Laoshan, Chefoo in the summers:
How did she do it? Without money? Arrange
excursions out of pestilent Shanghai?
The children play on the beach or hike
the mountain paths, while she cooks, cleans,
washes other people's clothes, sews, wheels and deals.
She laughs when they ask her: Mama, how did we live?
Her children, all white-haired today, who exchange
anxious glances over her head. And they say?
What fun those days, in Tsingtao, Chefoo, Laoshan!

Night eases into the garden.
The persimmons glow in the dusky tree.
She is thinking of Harbin's frozen drifts,
Vladimir and the others with vodka, speeches, tears.

And she is back, back across the Ussuri,
midnight and muffled oars, to Khabarovsk,
always back to those lost wooden houses,
smoke rising in the cold like breaths;
back to where her small daughters wait
in the dusk that is always falling
on her gracious mother,
her white-bearded father
waving in the doorway.

Just before Katya comes
to take her in for supper,
she is west on the Trans-Siberian,
across taiga, the Urals, the steppes,
to Smolensk, snow drifting in the streets,
then up to Velikije Luki, sleepy hamlet, a summer

long before the Revolution, before the Nazi slaughter.
She smiles at the birch swing in the grove
of birches, at her young parents who have met
today, forsaking others, their love tossing
aside arrangements and conventions, not long
before her own conception, fateful
intersection now vanished
from all maps:
Gno, 1895.

Re-Unions

85th Birthday

We are gathered from the far-flung reaches
of the globe: Maria's children come
to celebrate her life.

A special service in the Russian church:
when was the last time I attended
any church? My kids glance

askance at the black-bearded priests
swinging incense burners, chanting,
singing in Great-Grandma's language.

The priests' rich tones, dark hymns,
incense, ornate icons, the liturgy
washes over us all, dissolves distances.

Here we stand together, one family
filling this small church, diverse
people sprung from one slight woman.

A singular shaft of sunlight
in a window shines on her old
old hands as they rest
on young Walter's dark
Salvadorian head.

2
90th Birthday

The banner draped across the house front
in Santa Barbara has pinned to it the flags
of several countries. Ah, Russian Diaspora.
We gathered again, yet another year.

Now saying good-bye on the front lawn,
this clear blue July day in California.
Good-bye to the Aussies! The Canucks!
The Yanks scattered from Florida to Minnesota
to California up the coast. Salvadorians.

We are all chattering, hugging, crying,
promising to write, until Katya tells us:
"Mama's at the window."
There she stands,
blessing us.

We'll meet like this again
in five years, we say.
In Australia, someone suggests,
for the Aussie part of the family.
We say this. What we don't say,
is in our tears.

3
The Last

Four years later we meet
in the city of tombstones
on the hills above San Francisco.
Here nations are divided as ever:
Italians, the Jews, Armenians,
Greeks, the Serbians, within borders
for once undisputed, yet overcrowded.

Even here our Russian parents rest
displaced, in a Serbian grave.

What fills me is how the fog
has lifted, how sunlight gleams on her
white hair, so alive there, just before
the lid closes and she's lowered in above
Vladimir, and how I never could, will
never now cross over to her on the far
banks of that mythic Volga River.

Natasha

Ainsi, toujours poussés vers de nouveaux rivages...
de Lamartine

You sail the Yellow Sea, Tsingtao relinquished,
Shanghai inexorably hauling the tramp.

Curled like a puppy among the bales of chopsticks,
the coiled ropes, salt, tar, fishy odors
in your nostrils as the long winds flap and flutter
your roof. You sleep stars sliding away, breathe
on the ocean's breast.

Sibir's snowbanks cradled you once.
Russia's birches whispered your name –
Natasha – to October's blue stare.

Now, deckside traveller, a feast is spread fit for Tsars
overthrown! A boy strums a guitar, voices sing love
songs to the passing night. The moon knows no boundary.
Like you, it sails illimitable realms.

Daughter of the taiga and the snow.
All the countries that smolder in your eyes!
Restless, you move from room to room,
drawing love's warm blankets over the child
sleeping down tomorrow's casual goodbye.

The smother of tropical nights, migraine
nights when you haunt the hallways, sing
every Russian song you can remember.
Do you think all your children are asleep?

Mama dancing, scarves in turmoil,
children whirling all around you,
you give us ocean depths and fiery stars.

And after all our frangipani madness,
into the storm's vacuum, your voice steals:
It is an Ancient Mariner, and he stoppeth one of three . . .
or maybe Poe's: *Suddenly, there came a tapping . . .*
or you choose to quote, again: *O lac . . .*
or read from bitter Maxim's *Mother.* See?
All the world's a stage, child, darling mine.

So I sail with you, Natasha, the unseen
future listening, while you swing legs aft
over the white spray furling behind the ship.

Laugh, sing your songs, make eyes at the boy
who leans forward, cupping your young hand
with his own sheltering a small flame in the night.

He too will be left behind, stories in the shadows.
Toss those chopsticks overboard, one by one.
See how they bob and trail for miles in the moon's
solace, bright and platinum wake.

Diaspora – Conception

In a continent where the wind
    smells of snow and orange groves,
and rivers born in ice perish
    deep in the mangroves, where tons
of mountain slide regularly after rain
    into the communal pain of hovels

I am conceived, a zygote, a polyglot
    of a zygote. I hear the Orinoco
ripple Spanish syllables
    native, but not native,
and then the native cry, tongue of
    the conqueror... conquered,

    but before I quite catch on,
my transparent fingers reaching for the flicker
of these many syllables, water and sun,

    the Volga thunders in
        a thousand horsemen
their wild whistles, wind in winter grass
    – or is it mother singing and weeping? –
and I can hardly bear this warm confinement,
lurching and kicking, seeking the way out
    into snow and the living cold.

    But wait, the Liffey whispers,
    strokes ancient walls and nudges voices
like balls tossed back and forth intelligently
    in the dark. I'm stunned into stillness.

These, too, are familiar:
the kiss of the North Sea on cold sand,
a high blue sky which pierces,
the deep moan of a ship in fog.

Oh Mother, Conmingler of rivers,
who has gathered up the continents
and in one final spasm
emptied into Germany's rubble.
I am cold and the syllables here
    march and bark.

Bad Canstatt (1952)

The first snows of that year
swarming down upon the ruins
gave the jumbled city pause.

A woman paced the streets,
dreamt sunlight glazed the slate
roofs and turrets of home.

Another waiting on a corner,
toes cramped with cold,
dreamt a porcelain bowl
of the purest white eggs.

A tethered pig in the hospital
courtyard rooted and rooted
in the black half-frozen mud.

Two stories up a determined nun
held out the squalling newborn:
"Here's your baby come to see you!"
Oh Mama, refugee,
displaced beyond belief,
still groggy, saying,
"Open the door, then.
Let her in."

Born Stateless

1

Not all are born with the tags of nations
hanging bloody from umbilical cords.

Let the old emigrees die with mother
country bitter on their tongues, clenched
in teeth, fading fields and mountains.

You ask my nationality. Don't. I'm weary
of fabrication, and you, native son, can't
quite comprehend this state of being born
stateless in a world riven with states.

Why wear Africa, a sliver of gold,
around my neck?
So you will ask.

2

White and freckled, the child cried, Why can't we
be citizens? Why can't we belong?

Frail conceptions of what *white race* meant,
of history's black chains bleeding the green
jungles. With growing conceptions of what
white race meant in her green and tumbled jungles,
in the warm spill of moonlight, in the mosquito whine
of the night, in highlife drumbeat and jangle voices along
backroads payday, in women's songs echoing down
secret jungle tunnels, hibiscus, frangipani, mango mango
    sweetoh,

in steam billowing off hot tar roads, in flooded rivers molten
    red,
in the storms' violent contortions.

In laughter, belly laughter, rollicking laughter, fall down
on the ground laughter, dance of laughter, thrumming,
jangling highlife laughter in the village, oh, oh Africa, Africa,
black eyes in laughter, belly laughter, laughter in the circle of
    earth
stamped in the schoolyard, stamped bare with laughter,
    breathless
laughter, hug-shaped laughter, you are my sister forever, you
    will
leave us laughter, you can't be one of us laughter, you are so
    white
laughter, oh laughter can you see my teeth clenched
    laughter, oh,
Africa shaped like a question mark, when will you have the
    answer?

                            3
Miners' camp in an equatorial night. Families sleep outside
    on the ground
too hot in the zinc-roofed company barracks. In a circle of
    light, small
children squat for the day's meal around a large almost
    empty cooking pot
of rice and greens. Their eyes glow soft as night, sparkle like
    water, their bellies taut, hugely round, navels jutting.

A giant man sits on a stool in the cool circle of lamplight.
Muscles weary, all day he's sweating labour in the mine –
    70% iron in that ore,

richest in the world – for eleven cents an hour. His woman
   rubs his shoulders and massive neck, his large gleaming
   bald head. On his knees he dandles an infant, his deep
   voice cooing like a village dove.

Into the deep wells missionaries shout the love
of Christ. Young boys spit
whisper of guns.

                              4
Don't ask my nationality; isn't it enough
to have been born?

   Periphery.

Circling New York she stares down into canyons
bathed in the strange orange glow
of a northern summer dusk.

In La Guardia the younger children have discovered
escalators. Up and down, endlessly they travel
terribly pleased, but she, so old already,
must watch the suitcases, while her harried mother
argues the next plane.

And then a woman in African dress walks by,
her head held erect, draped West African style.
Suddenly the girl on the suitcase is blinded.
Her mother finds her drowning and can't save her.

I wear Africa, a sliver of gold
around my neck.

5

Joseph sings as he washes dishes. He leaves
perfect circles of black hair in the bathroom
sink when he combs his head and surveys his smile
in the mirror.

Joseph sits behind the house to study.
He is Africa, studying studying.
"One meal a day," he says, "is all I need." He's
handsome as a mahogany tree in the forest,
wealthy with country. I squat beside him
in the thin shadows of afternoon.

I watch his eyes as they fly the pages.
His cheeks are stippled with young beard,
and when he smiles the sky dances, the sun
wheels madly for the dimples in his cheeks

until that early morning when I walk
into the kitchen dressed only in my underwear,
and Joseph is already there working.
He stares for one long grim moment and back
again to my mother's sinkful of dishes.
"Get dressed," he growls, his tone a punch
whirling me around, and I flee,
hot shame, sudden knowledge like amoeba
multiplying in my twelve year old gut.

Where are you now, my childhood
love, sweet smile in that land soaked
in blood, where are you now? Where guns speak
and machetes hack out the very heart of Africa?

6

Oh, West Africa, wealthy in moonlight and children,
green rain forests glittering sun, lashed red sinews
of rivers, muscles flexing, muscles torn, new chains.

Closing my eyes, I hear the women still
singing in the forests, see them cast nets
into those tenebrous creeks, their wet bodies
swaying as they lift the wriggling fish high.

And you, sister of my childhood, Georgia, your name
descended from freed slaves reposited on Africa's
shore: Freeman! Where are you? That noon sun never
cast shadows on us, the bared circle of schoolground
where we all stamped our feet in the dancing game.
That patch'll never grow grass again! How your green
turban set off your skin! Green lapa and buba queen!
Sisters – but now I know. All our songs and dances,
hands clapping rhythms, forest trails we skipped,
all these were yours, not mine, now I know.
The child sunk, bitter the burden of her white skin.
Africa's coastline recedes.

I pressed your farewell beads to my lips
as the plane ascended and I grew lighter
and lighter, hollow, turned inside out,

a mere mote adrift in the darkness
over the Atlantic for hours formless.
My lovely sister Georgia, how I envied
you then the starry night of your skin.

7

Most are born with the tags of nations
possessive, dripping bloody from umbilicus

and in the long corridors and streets
the ancient celebratory echoes.

Toss-Up (1964)

Brazil?
Canada?
Canada.
Brazil.
Brazilia! Now there!
Kids! What a magnificent
city all planned! You'll love it.
You'll belong in no time.

But what about Canada?
They speak English in Canada.
We don't know Portuguese.
And the boys are already
in school there. Couldn't we
belong to Canada?

Still, think: warm tropics
as we're used to.
Could we bear to live in such
cold as they do in Canada?

Canada?
Brazil?
Brazil… uh oh…
A military coup!
Soldiers in the streets.
Overthrow…

Canada.
Yes, Canada.

Leaving Africa (1965)

Yards from the fence at the airfield
the broad black river reflects
jungle, a canoe, heaped clouds.

With my little box camera I'm busy
capturing the river, the thatched village
across the water, zinc roofs flashing sun.

The canoe with a woman and boy slips
upriver to where crocodiles slumber
in the shallows: I've seen them.

Along the web of paths carved
into the far bank women sway,
burdens balanced delicately,

while kids arch their fiery bodies
into the water, their cries taut
bowstrings quivering.

Behind me, voices call.
Ignore them.
The plane can leave without me.
This river vein spilled from the Bomi Hills'
high teak forests torn, uprooted,
water iron-rich as blood,

down, down in foaming rapids through
jungle to the dunes' buttress
against the Atlantic – how can I go?

As he hurries me across the grass
he looks up, my kid brother, and asks,
"Can I please carry your camera?"

I let him. Somewhere between Dakar
and Toronto, the camera is lost.

South of Bloor (1965)

Days off the trans-Atlantic flight
from Africa's warm coasts,
we trudge the streets of Toronto.
    Where shall we live?

The July air so cold,
our sweaters not enough
to warm our thin tropic blood

as we walk, Mama and her six kids,
little hen with chicks,
strange sidewalks, leering houses,
porches grey peeling paint,
open front doors dark gullets,
smells that float out, cling
to our nostrils as we flee
the odours of cat and decay.

I remember I wondered:
Is this where those American kids
came from? Places like these?

Those kids in the mining camp
who wore sneakers and jeans and boasted
about "Stateside" or "Back Home."
I'd always imagined Dick and Jane
on Cherry Lane.

But the truth! Such sour streets!
For Rent signs in windows, alleys
garbage-strewn. Had they played tag

in cramped corner parks lush
with green glass shards, where old
grizzled men snore under newspapers?

Oh Mama! Why have we come here?

We straggle back to the strangers
whose floors we sleep upon.
That old ex-missionary sputters:
Not south of Bloor! You shouldn't
have gone looking south of Bloor!

But, in memory of Cherry Lane,
how were we to know?

Milk

Milk.
Cold. In tall glasses.
As much as you can drink.

Milk.
In each hand
a three quart jug.

Milk.
Four little kids eager
to fetch it home.

That first milk
in Canada. We could
not get enough.

Daily across the cobblestones
of Bloor Viaduct we swung
our empty jugs in hand,

six quarts each day.
Mama could've bought a cow.

First Snow

tropical night a mystery of shrieks and pipings
trees scuffle in the odoriferous wind
melodious, dissonant
yet the heart lending rhythm

Our eyes wide wide
we listen for the rain to sweep in
and someone asks Mama
  Well, what is winter like, then?

Her voice over by the window:
  Imagine living in a huge freezer
  frost in your bones... chilly, oh!

We shudder in our beds, giggling, until Bobby says,
  But what about frogs and crickets?
  What about the lizards? Huh?

I wonder aloud, *What does snow really look like?*
Over by the window Mama slowly says
  What does it look like?
and we wait, not a peep, hold our breaths.

Suddenly her laughter catches in the dark
  like fire.
Termites when they swarm and swirl
in columns at street lamps, or in car headlights
... sometimes snow looks like that.

We hear her sigh, huge sigh,
    see her outlined in lightning
count for thunder… crackles by two.

But one night, months later, cold
across the ocean, our illusions scrunched
underfoot, Canada, oh Canada, nothing
like we'd dreamed, the boys yell from outside:
    Hey everyone, it's snowing!

I rush out barefoot, terrified
electric joy.
See a huge hushed opalescent sky,
no stars… feel on my face
cold kisses.

Origins

1

"Spare," you said of the poems,
"be more spare."

Pare this fleshy mango to the stone.
Hone – chisel – whittle – slice
like north wind in snow.

Permission to express this
country cracked, sunblistered, peeling
yellow old skin in strips
                    or
            incised blue granite
lyrical
                    as hoarfrost
birches.
            Try thistles,
    Canada or sow,
                    sow-thistle
            sound yellow?
prickly enough?
            Purple more troublesome?
                    Then say *Canada*.
            Native of Europe,
Creeping Thistle,
alien here, but most widespread,
            did you know
that?

Wild oats,
black random eyes in the tame grain,
whatever
            ice to the flush of fever
may help
      this blood thicken in time,
blood as Africa in flood.
      O thunder! O crash of rain!
on small roofs mimetic of palm trees
frenetic fronds
      castanet gypsy in the child
wild in the woman
      old chaos again crawls out
            released

whipped red hibiscus
            frangipani rampant in the rain!

      when all dictates excess
suck in *suck sing* succinct

Spare! Be more spare!
pare that poetic diction
to the bone.

Under the shadowing panoply of jungle carved
by a creek, the child crouches on a boulder,
watches fisherwomen ripple the pools below
with wide shimmering sweeps of small nets.

Clad only in black bikini pants and green
shadows, they murmur laughter like water
over pebbles, weaver birds, the softly-softly
in the evening trees, their brown breasts like bells.

How be spare?
Lost in that dusky jungle
where I sit, concealed.

Conversations

Waves of words,
tides pulled and pushed
by that great moon:
our affinitive existence.

Never ask for a paraphrase.

I could summon only the swells
of amusement in my throat.

Oh my poet, grey matter
so finely encased!
Cells, blood, bone, marrow;
a scent that shafts
to sudden casualties
my most sensible intentions.

Each nuance a snowflake
stealing the dark night.

I hear your words
and pain to touch your skin
beyond, tongue the hidden ache
of your genesis.

Impossibilities are thus cherished,
nurtured, embers blown bright
with extrapolations.

Goodnights always arrive
as dull surprises.

Black Creek Pioneer Village

The white pine timber walls astound
me with their weight, sheer massive
arrogance of the hewer in this
superfluity of wood
enclosing a candle flame.

I lean my ear
to the smoky gleam of wood
and hear above the moan
of winter
the muffled thump
of blood.

Immigrant Kids

"I had kinda a rough time,"
Paolo confided laughingly.

We lay on the hot sand,
Wasaga Beach, July, 1968,

this young bronze god,
his hand on my belly.

How I listened to his mouth.

"See, I almost starved as a baby."

Small Italian village
deep in parched mountains
where ancient trails led
nowhere anymore,
after the war,
and before I was born
Paolo was already starving,
his mama crying, Papa's jaw
steel-edged.

I gathered it all up in his brown
eyes even as he laughed.

"So when we came to Canada,
my parents stuffed me so much,
I got real fat."
We cried laughing.

E.S.L. Class

Grief drips like honey
from the smashed honeycomb.
Every face is stamped

upon, treads visible
if you know how to look.

Flimsy vessels – we strained against
oceans bursting in.
I left behind my brother.

He marches on and on into the snows
across mountains – always January.
A bullet in the back still aches.

We rode horses all night
into the highest mountain pass.
Near the border in a storm
I lost my sister.

She, motherhood buried
in the blood-rust soil
of several continents, breaks
into a slight rocking motion
when she speaks.

Honey like grief.

Our land spread golden sea
to sea to sea.

Desert Briefing

So begins the mourning
cerulean, cerise
contrails, entrails
red mist

and every morning she gathers up
rough contours of flesh, breath, beard
burn crimson on her cheeks
rumpled blankets, biceps, belly
swirled hair, her face thrust
into the armpit odour of his blue shirt
she breathes and breathes in
the shock of that last sock buried
in the sofa cushions
the photos still
in the camera.

"With the Republican Guards decimated,
the casualties will be few."

ABC's Sam Donaldson, Jan., 20, 1991
Saudi Arabia

New Century

Blue gradations into brown haze.
The city suspires and somewhere
else, a million expire... but not here
where February yawns sunshine
in wide brown-mottled fields,
ice-puddle lawns. Kids fling open
coats, drive skate blades
through slush.

Lucky kids!
Keep skating.

Somewhere else
the sky is falling
and falling.

Jorge

to the memory of Jorge Alberto Martinez,
construction worker, husband, father
murdered by the fascists, 1982, El Salvador

1

The critic smiles, "Such blatant accusations:
fascist murderer, imperialist puppet,
are inappropriate, have no place in poetry."
He doodles little blank faces, mustachioed,
and tiny question marks, sardonic
in the margins of my rage.
Understatement the soul of… Remember?

2

A tiny flower embroidered on the blue shirt
Maritza stitched with smiling anticipation
of the pleasure sure to be in Jorge's dark eyes,
and on that morning he wore the shirt, flower
blooming above his heart.

But she hadn't known how dangerous he was.
Only the warm flesh filling her with child,
his quiet joy at the growing minor earthquake
moving against his broad builder's palms
spread like a benediction on her belly.

But supposedly he was dangerous!
On the February morning when they came for him,
becoming so.

54

And the night – all the days one hellish night –
resounds with the heart's rhythm of terror:
Mi amor, mi alma, mi vida,
where are you? What have they done?

Each day La Puerta del Diablo swings
open for her beneath skies crowded
and reeling with drunken vultures,
as she searches, screaming the glutted dogs
away from half-gnawed corpses.
She searches in the stench of rotting flesh,
discarded scraps from the butcher's slab.

Silently the people come,
casting no shadows in that sun,
picking over the dangerous garbage.
Is it him? At last? This pitiful scattered scrawl?
How can this be?
Such an epitaph for his violated dignity!

Oh, but poet,
remember the understatement
inherent in poetry.
Don't shout: fascist murderers!
Don't scream: imperialist puppets!
No, no, whisper like the softly rising wind
whispers through the severed sequences of limbs.

She haunts the dumping grounds
sick with dread that she will find him,
when she doesn't, ill with relief.
So many have stumbled forward,
their cries strangling in recognition.

She walks among the bodies and the bones,
glancing into torn and frozen grimaces,
wounds and orifices white with maggots spilling,

until that morning glistening in El Playon,
the sun just hazy rising in the trees,
when she arrives alone and sees
clouds of vultures proclaiming another feast
of human flesh abundantly heaped.

Even from the distance,
before she sees his eyes have been gouged,
the seething black blooms
where his ears used to be,
the bullet holes… *Dios mio…*
her man's bloody black castration,

through the hot eruption of tears she sees
the pale blue shirt she stitched so carefully,
the little flower.

In My Uncle's House

In my uncle's house in Frisco,
back then, the walls had a way
of expanding as the rooms filled
with those seeking refuge:

El Salvador's loss, America's gain.
All those young people who came
flooding into my uncle's home,
my *tia* welcoming yet another
nephew or cousin's son,

my uncle never once forgetting
his own past statelessness, his
seventeen-year-old self at the port
of no return, portholes revealing
fog, endless sky or ocean
heaving to what seemed an infinity
of the unknown.

And then, finally, to see an official
waiting, hands imperiously thrust out:
"Your papers please."

No, one never forgets the fear
in the pit of the belly, the dry-mouthed,
choked exhilaration of safe entry.

Delta

Face
eroded eloquent
around the eyes.

The hands speak:
nations, tribes, clans:
so much earth descending amid
the harsh weeping of women.

She has not borne her son's silken body
nor her daughters', waves and hills,
to release them for slaughter.
A *curve of cheek silk to my palm.*

In the morning she walks out into the sky
tremendous over the fields,
the first human,
and the sky is an ocean
feathered with blood.

The Death of Sardanapalus

October in Paris on a day for umbrellas.
Yesterday, in weather cool and sunny, I visited
Baudelaire's grave in Montparnasse. At his tomb
numerous bus tokens, scraps of poems, small love
notes, wilted flowers, and propped against the stone
a large laminated sketch of the poet himself. Offerings.
My homage only fragments remembered: *J'entends déjà
tomber avec des chocs funebres... tomber...* logs tumbling
in a cobblestoned courtyard, nineteenth century chill
autumn night, the poet's red and frozen heart –
He's buried here as simply someone's son.

Had you also visited this hallowed spot? *You.*
I bowed my head invoking sadness, but looking up,
caught the glance of another, a daypack slung
over one shoulder. He nodded, edged away, was gone.
Deserted, I stared down at the stone, the names
and dates inscribed, all the paper offerings.
Lovers of poetry. Offerings of lovers.
You? Your name evoked nothing. In the distance
workmen were uprooting a bed of flowers.

A faint sense of futility now accompanied
my tour: Samuel Beckett, Simone and Jean Paul,
Marguerite Duras. On all their graves
flowers, fresh and withering.

Today, walking in the rain towards the Louvre, I could hear
Baudelaire, in some smoke-roughened voice: *Tout l'hiver
va rentrer dans mon être.* In Paris a week now, I could no
longer avoid what you'd obsessed about all those years

ago. You said you'd sat for hours in contemplation
before the huge Delacroix. And because I'd adored
your amazing eyes as you spoke of the painting,
the very image of you sitting alone in the gallery
among crowds, eyes pensive black, chin cupped in hands,
every step I took closer to the Louvre
brought you back to me, until, surprised, in some relief,
I felt that ancient pain suffuse each cell.

You crossed this bridge, leaned over watching
barges on the Seine, water jostling, splitting light. You
touched this very balustrade… My fingers stroked rough
stone. *But, love, I've always had suspicions*
about your Sardanapalus.

In the gallery of the huge paintings, I found the bench
in front of the painting where you'd sat ten years ago.
Crowds moved restlessly. Behind me *Liberty Leading the*
    People,
I gazed up at *The Death of Sardanapalus.* The enormity of it.
As you'd described. I plumbed my sense of awe
at the carnage depicted – *my god, my god* – close
to examine details, brush stroke and line, then away
to the bench again. *Why?* This little word like carbonated
bubbles surfacing. I wished *why* would prick like the tip
of a sword poised to slice my heart open. Yet I took notes
like some schoolgirl or journalist. I wrote:

The carnage a metaphor, bloodless: amid the sumptuous
    wealth
daggers plunge in veils of hair, silk, fleshy curves – languor,
    not death,
a thousand times rehearsed, the woman half-disrobed, face
    down

on the edge of his bed, arms out-stretched like one
    completely sated,
or crucified, and there on the margins, the surprised horse
whose shoulder has just swallowed a sword.

Only in shadows can one see the dagger wound self-inflicted
on a slave's chest. Light links the flesh of those offered up,
a path lit to Sardanapalus himself reclined in shadow,
    detached,
yet central to the slaughter, all lines drawn to his grim visage.
No one can tell what he sees or who, or if he sees at all the
    toll
and embraces it. There is no blood. So the enemy has gained
the citadel. At what is Sardanapalus gazing? The destruction
of his loved possessions as he ordered? Why did he order it
    so?
Defence? Revenge? *What had you seen, darling one?* Love?
Or death by supreme indifference?

My Country

Foreign to these rhythms, hoping to arrive
anonymous at half-past eight, I find
the crowd arrives at ten. I've come
for you, my country.

I imagine you're everywhere
imminent. Can't help but stare at each
new stranger greeted at the door.

Through the huge window I watch the lake
darken, lights pearl on the water, occasional
sparks as a trout leaps. You must be somewhere
beyond the platinum moon. Can't you hear
the night spill over?

Why did I think you'd come? I'm so foreign!
You'd be amazed at my coherence in a dozen
conversations! So much laughter, brittle
brilliance, no intonations of that exile,
ill for you, my country.

Firelight, firelight,
plays like breath and fingers
on the dark and golden
contours of my country

soft, insistent beard
brush against my throat
across my mouth sighing
oh, my country . . .

Citizen

Fresh snow a mother of pearl
on the old volcano.

The wind down the valley
evokes the sea.

Eyes closed I float,
a moat in the current

of sunshine, and open
to see my country.

Once in fragments strewn
on every continent,

I didn't know who stared
back in mirrors. But today…

I overheard someone say
he'd spoken of me.

Bow River in May

By the river, early evening,
I hum Russian tangos
to myself, and strains
of Tchaikovsky's Sixth.
High alps in snow glow
the last sun.

This swiftly-rising water too obvious
a metaphor, relentlessly gaining
in depth and velocity within
the hour – no matter how
intensely I may wish it,
you don't appear.

Later, wandering the streets,
seeking you in the drinking spots,
I peer in like some shy kid
sent to find her father, or brother,
and have to back out quick from the heat,
smoke and voices, animated stares.

This twinkling evening,
tourist town – dear god!
That in mere days
I've forgotten
how to be
alone.

Runner

Were I ten years younger,
my heart would be entirely frantic,
lost to you, marvellous boy.
I wouldn't be able to bear
breathing the same casual air.

So finely tuned,
attuned,
you tautly strung harp,
what music!

God pity the young girl
who forgets to exhale
when you smile,
when you speak,
you lovely Greek!

Faces like yours
graced the Parthenon,
debated with Socrates,
poured over volumes at Alexandria,
climbed in thunder and sun to Delphi.

Trained at Sparta.

Runner in the dark mountains,
the wars make fierce demands.
Compelled to run such distances,
messenger, lungs bursting,
God, look at you!
Come lay your tender head
down in this woman's lap.
I've ten years on you.
I can say it.

Migrant

The Sunday park dreams in Spanish.
Drowsy sycamore shade,
rustles in an arid breeze,
flickers in the central stillness:
a young man, dark rolled in shadows,
buries his head in his arms.

Sometimes there sit two like him,
smiling shyly at children chasing frisbees,
and mothers chasing babies,
and sometimes in the evening,
when stars tremble in the leaves,
he becomes a whole circle, ringing
a guitar and softly singing.

October Straits

I've watched age creep into my mother's face,
heard her voice spring from my throat,

clung to the notion of my children leaping
endlessly forward, like young deer in tangled
forests of moments.

I'd even embraced my own statelessness,
and thought only death now
could have undone me,

until this theft across a café table,
where, intently, a spy, an artist
hungering, I memorized your face,
and suddenly noticed, beyond
the smoothing of my fingers,
that faint indelible tracery.

Bereft, borderless, fog-soft night
of ferry engines booming as I seek
the railing farthest from the light,

and all around into the darkness
hundreds of little waves clash,
shatter white hisses.

Varykino 1

We are the only ones now
For the walls of logs to regard in melancholy
We made no promises to storm barricades
We shall go down to perdition openly
                    Pasternak, "Autumn" Zhivago

1

After a poem by Chagall

His homeland lay within him –
by turns the birch forest leaning
in carved wooden windows
(mushroom picking, *white flash of limbs*),
and the village's long crooked street,
grey weathered fences – silver combs
parting the green lush of gardens.

He waited in the Paris parks,
arms outstretched for snow, cold
kisses on his upturned face.
When he felt lonely, sometimes she came,
his homeland, and tucked him into sleep.

Eighty years he cast exulting spirits
over the departed houses of his childhood:
blue cows, red roosters or green, delighted angels
sent to eavesdrop; once he flew himself, his body
encircling the moon, blue over Vitebsk,
hands clutching flowers.

Like that other one, Nabokov, chasing rare butterflies
in summer meadows long before the treads of tanks

zippered up the earth; they could do this, artists
in exile who carried their childhood like precious

sheaves of wheat grown only in that soil.

They took what they needed when they fled, and so
preserved the language of birches, village houses
with carved wooden windows, crooked lanes,
icons of childhood, like Chagall's Vitebsk,
ninety-three percent obliterated for the rest
of us, one way or another, Stalin or Hitler,
Hitler – Stalin.

2

Poets/Places

Was Chagall that winding village street,
weathered fences leaning slightly sunken?
His eye caught the warm auras of houses
long gone…

Somewhere a crooked street – Mandelstam –
wrenched out of stone beside the river.
Stand there for a while, darlings,
observe the burial of the sun.

In cold Leningrad Anna rejects
the Summer Garden, queues
near the clanging prison gate.
Lean now, another age, on a stone
balustrade, watch the snow flakes drown
in the Neva.

Marina's path – bitter exile and return –

she occupied the very pain inhaled by a whole
generation, yet none saw her final slow sway
and swivel from the nail.

On the other side of town Mayakovsky gathers
all the seas high into his embrace, clouds too,
continents and voices; he's the oceans' foam.
Hear him spill through chasms

and then grieve for the child perched
on the broad shoulders of the crowd,

that winsome child, swinging
on the garden's gate.

Varykino 2

Thief . . .
    why did they
call me *thief?*

I hear Anna's scorn
even now; how she refused
to see me, though he,
the other half,
was always welcome.

*Stealing another woman's man
and worse* (a winter of a wife
he'd never leave).
I was the warm he sheltered in,
the season unlocking the river.

I blew on his cold fingertips,
and suddenly language gushed.

Who owns the air, can steal
sunlight or clouds?

Remember this, all of you, eager,
hefting stones from palm to palm.

Could it be our Lord Himself
set us on our convergent paths?

2

In the wilderness a pear tree
flowered, its trunk skirted
with lush aromatic grasses.

Alone it stood, its white blossoms
a reproach to sterility.

3

But you now, my love, what landscape?
What rare combination will suffice for the bare
bones of the country swathed in ermine?

Can snow be warm enough? Can a country survive
a spine so exposed, each vertebra a polished
cobblestone? (Or *keys on a flute* the wind owns?)

No, I wouldn't hang this one on you.
I still have you – warm skin and tears.
I still wear your rasp on my cheeks.
When I shut my eyes I have you,
mornings, bleary from the candles'
smoke; all night you held the country
in your arms warm as blood and whispered
Come on, *malinkaya,* come on, breathe!

4

If you are a place at all,
you're Varykino, wooden dacha,
homestead smoke just over the next
rise in the taiga,

hidden in the labial folds of earth,
birch woods like fine hair static
in the pale wash of winter sky,

nearby the ravine where in summer
the poet lay, dust and bullet-bitten.
How flies halo his words! Somewhere
a woman still weeps.

My Varykino! In the cities' arteries
we check our pulses, accept daily infusions
of war and grief; on the street corner
the old proffer the last silver spoon,
the last blackened icon handed down.

Hieroglyphic snow geese in the winter
fields cry for the south where spring's
crushed beneath tank treads.

Alas! The woodcutters have fled the forests;
peasants have left their crops rusting in the fields.
Abandoned, mice frolic nightly in the pans
and pots and fallen armour: clink, clank, clink.
When I close my eyes, I hear them play.
You beside me in the dark: barely a breath.
Are you?   There.

Once summer tossed sun and wind
into your stubbled face. We could've
planted that victory garden, the soil
rich, untouched.

But winter! Oh, my hard-boned one.
The blue nights, the small fire, the candle
sputters, a tiny rage.

5

They came for me, love, to confirm
your criminal nature.
I told them. How could I hide

what you've done to me? Shaken
to the core. *Yes, he tore away the bindings,*
rolled the boulder from the door.

When had I first met you? loved you?
What meeting? Where? When? Who else
was present? Who else had memorized
your poems?

Those sorry souls…
      it wasn't poems they were after
this time.
      Secretly I laughed
to think of *Lara* safe
in someone's lap in an Italian piazza!
All those fountains! That sun!

Day after day they kept on
asking the same questions: would I change
my story? But truth is mutable only
under torture; they remained polite.

When I was a young girl and he
      an image in a book, a rumour breathing
lilacs, a voice cleaving the green wheat.

I walked in the woods, your books clasped
to my childish breasts: *how could he*
know me so well? In a meadow
        your poems like burrs
            or thorns.

But I understood only half and craved the other
as a hooked fish craves the brook.

   He's a god who can
   speak like this.

Forgive me
but I
said
nothing.

The hours trickle.
In the midnight sun of a light bulb
they come to question us about everyone.

Deep within me our child skips.
I thought no one knew he existed,
not even you, poking his toes under my ribs,
tracing my heart as with a fine paper edge,
each stroke blood-beaded.
I think of pigeons
in the patch of sky
beyond the bars,

the flutter-kisses
of your lashes.

The other women lie on cots,
kerchiefs shielding their eyes.
"Try and sleep", they say, "better
for the baby." So you see?
Nothing is hidden
Mary Magdalen.

6

Late at night they came to the cell.
"We are taking you to him,"
they smiled. My heart crashed
upward, a fish in rapids.
"To him," they said.
Could you have come for me?
The night so blessed with rainy air,
I took great gulps, was tossed
into a police van.

The Lubianka . . .
      unfolding
nightmare
      countless
corridors they led me,
            sleepwalker,
up spirals, down, our steps
   hollow.
I realized they were lying.

     Down down at last
as into catacombs, the air
   danker with each step.
Where are you taking me? I asked my keepers. *Where
  is he whom my soul loveth?*

Their silence tightened my arms
　　around our hidden infant.
At last a door, a wave of cool air.
　　They shoved me forward
and clanked it shut, were gone.
Love. Into the gloom I peered. Of course
　　　　you were not there.
　　　　　　I refused
to think you were one of those
　　shrouded on the tables... puddles, water
　　　　or blood, on the whitewashed floor
　　the sweetish odour –
　　　　　　God help me

　　Hush. Why seek him here?
　　　He is arisen.

Yet I sank to the floor
my feet in a puddle
our child turned over
in horror, beat at my walls
with tiny fists and heels,
clawed at that coffin lid.

We had a son.
For a few weeks he ran gaily
like a little mouse
in the round of my ribs.

Return to Varykino

We're finally here,
yet I keep asking myself,
Why this deserted place?

Desert place . . .
winter seeps in through chinks
next to the bed, chill breath,
while across the room you
hunch over the table,
intense candle.

Your pen hovers, a kestrel
above the white steppes.

You think I'm asleep,
your face so unguarded.

The fire-logs slump and sink.
Have we burnt all the wood
already? Frost arches on the window
beyond your silhouette,
god! so beloved.

One hand plunged into your hair,
you blow warmth on the other,

until the flame gutters. You rise,
a shadow to the window
frost-ferns in moonlight now,
breathe a peephole to peer out
at our country littered
with stars.

Come, at last,
your feet icy on my warm skin.
Keep reminding me.

2

I couldn't sleep.
God knows I measured
each breath you took and
slowed my own until I thought
I'd never breathe again.

Don't expect this woman
to take bread for granted.
Oh no, how could I

sleep? With your slumbering warmth
wedged between me and night,
I wanted to memorize each breath
on my neck, the hair on your arm, bones
in your wrist, the veins of your hand
on my breast, like a watershed
in Eden.

Shh… don't say I'm too damn
sentimental. I'm a child of the poet
slain in the ravine. Come,
let me tell you my dream.

I must have slept after all,
wakened only when you took
your body from mine
so carefully.
What is it you see from the window?
You're shivering. Come back –
the world keeps slipping
around in its bloody tracks.

I dreamt of men with guns, flames
leaping rivers, smoking villages we saw
from the train. A small girl was running
down a road, her body on fire, and in Moscow
all the church bells clanging
were women hanging.

Lie beside me
Varykino in snow.

3

We won't starve.
Not with this golden dog who's adopted us.
He knows where to poke his plundering nose
into snow drifts exactly below the tree
where October's pears lie frozen, sweet
sunlight in stilled molecules.

Thistles enclosed the garden.
Remember? The day you called.
I was all out of breath, denied it was
because of your voice laughing over the wire:
    When are you coming?

I'd rushed in from the cold.
Told you I'd been digging thistles
all afternoon, the toughest taproots.
We won't starve here, I wanted to say.
The soil is rich, thistles sky high.
I could hardly speak with the wind burn
in my throat closed as you spoke:
    Thistles? You're harvesting thistles?

4

The wind's voice edges hysteria as snow
descends with the dusk, a billion scuffling
flakes, and still the deer feed.

Look there in the field near the woods, barely
visible shapes defying the storm,
scraping snow from the corn.

Our country in winter,
slender ribs bared.

5

This was a mistake.
I can see it in the broad palm
prints you've left on the frosted pane.

The little room we've shared can't
hold all our desires, yet the rest
of the house, draped in hoarfrost,
belongs to someone else.

She's returning. I listen for the bells
of her sleigh in the snow.

6

We keep this troika on track, the three
   of us; endurance is the point,
      destiny a cat's cradle.
Look at us. Straining through the dusk,
snow like a cloud of locusts, or some careless
   tornado screaming eastward, we keep
      our eyes on track.

   Careful…
one slight tilt or hidden
   rut, we'll be flung
   shattering into each other,
 traces tangled, the only omen
that raven, a smear
   in the sky.

7

An explosion of deer
    from the brush, up the rise,
they split through the trees.
    How many? Five? Vanished.
We came too near: a scent of wolves.

8

Somewhere through these trees
is a small wall of logs chopped
into stove lengths, neatly stacked

and tucked between the trunks
of young oaks. I made note
of this before the snow. Old
lichen-encrusted logs, gnarled,
abandoned. How long ago? Who was
the woodcutter who placed each

chunk of wood with such care, knots
and curves aligned, tightly fit as
an old married couple asleep,
she half-hidden under his arm,
curled up, cheek on his chest,
stomach to hip, or knee to knee?
Something we will never be.

There it is, that comfortable stack,
well-built, enduring the weight
of all this snow . . .

A couple of kicks'll topple it.

9

You hold up the mirror
of your poems to my face.

In this magic glass
conjuror's wink,
a rawboned me transformed
into universal *she,*

as you rewrite our nerves and flesh.

She   the wind at the window
a small dog or ghost.

   I can't help wondering
about your wife...

and have to hide my hands; they are too
   rough, smell of onions
         and strong yellow soap.

All day I've polished my knuckles
   on the washboard; your damp shirts
sag the line bisecting the room

humid with my work;
the cold walls glitter.

I hum blue lullabies for the unborn
in the white winter night of our country.
   When has it not been winter?
Who are we to deserve such a bountiful
   season, whole centuries?

Yet without winter would we have needed
   such candles as we have witnessed
      flaming? Such candles!

The fire is dying slowly.
   I pretend to sleep
      as your pen scratches
  and scratches
     tiny chasms in me.

10

Nichevo.
In life as in art
you tricked me, your Larusha.

You bade me go for safety's sake,
and you'd follow.
But, love, when I turned to see,
you were distant in the snowy steppe,
waving and waving,
and that was the fiction.
How often I waited for you
to cross the furrowed field,
autumnal or wintry wood,
the little footbridge to my home,
and each good-night so final!

Now I've come to see you.
I dreamed you were calling me.
No one has seen me slip through
the door. Morning sun streaks
your face still warm, your hands soft,
shadows swarm across the floor,
old love, so many
   candles burning.

11

Your name still blows about the stars,
and like a torn leaflet in the streets,
catches the eye   snags the heart

What was it all for?

Youngsters in the alley below
barter their bodies and souls.

Perhaps you're asking, love,
Was it for this we were
slaughtered?

Over the Kremlin, tricolours again
(sky/blood/snow), triumphant
in the wind reeking of war.

No one agrees on who we are, love, a nation
of expatriates, of Cossacks, poets exiled,

gangsters or revolutionaries, proletariat or
slaves, artists within shifting borders,

we're stateless on the platform
waiting for the last train to Varykino.

12

She was but the mistress, they say,
old now, her room muttering...

All your scribbles I'd saved,
letters, books you'd inscribed:
    Olga, my Larissa,
captive in the vaults of our nation.

Never mind,
everything's memorized.

Dubious poet, hugging your private life...
    at a time like this!

Shh... you say, wrapping us warm.
They're only wolves howling
at the edge of the woods.
See? One clap of my hands
and they scatter.

Printed in
November 2004
at Gauvin Press Ltd., Gatineau, Québec